Comets

by Grace Hansen

Abdo
OUR GALAXY
Kids

abdopublishing.com

Published by Abdo Kids, a division of ABDO, P.O. Box 398166, Minneapolis, Minnesota 55439.

Copyright © 2018 by Abdo Consulting Group, Inc. International copyrights reserved in all countries. No part of this book may be reproduced in any form without written permission from the publisher.

Printed in the United States of America, North Mankato, Minnesota.

052017

092017

THIS BOOK CONTAINS
RECYCLED MATERIALS

Photo Credits: ESA, iStock, NASA, Science Source, Shutterstock

Production Contributors: Teddy Borth, Jennie Forsberg, Grace Hansen

Design Contributors: Dorothy Toth, Laura Mitchell

Publisher's Cataloging in Publication Data

Names: Hansen, Grace, author.

Title: Comets / by Grace Hansen.

Description: Minneapolis, Minnesota : Abdo Kids, 2018 | Series: Our galaxy |
    Includes bibliographical references and index.

Identifiers: LCCN 2016962402 | ISBN 9781532100505 (lib. bdg.) |
    ISBN 9781532101199 (ebook) | ISBN 9781532101748 (Read-to-me ebook)

Subjects: LCSH: Comets--Juvenile literature.

Classification: DDC 523.44--dc23

LC record available at http://lccn.loc.gov/2016962402

Table of Contents

How Comets Formed

Our **solar system** formed around 4.6 billion years ago. Gravity combined dust and gas over millions of years. This is how the sun was created.

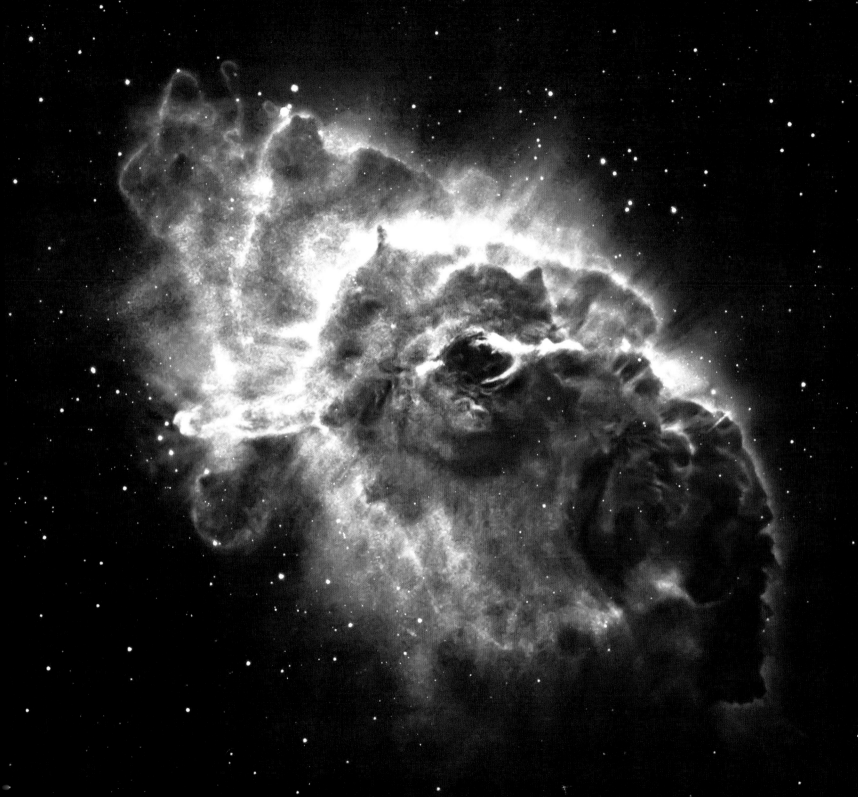

5

Dust and gas then began to **orbit** the sun. They collided and formed lumps. Many lumps formed far from the sun's heat. Some of those lumps became comets.

The Nucleus

Each comet has a **nucleus**.
The nucleus is made up of
ice, frozen gases, and dust.

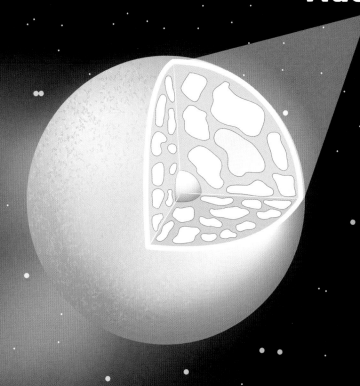

Nucleus

Nucleuses range in size. Smaller ones can be the size of a house. Larger ones can be more than 6 miles (9.7 km) across!

11

There are short- and long-period comets. Short-period comets have **orbits** that take less than 200 years to complete. They come from the Kuiper belt and the **scattered disc**.

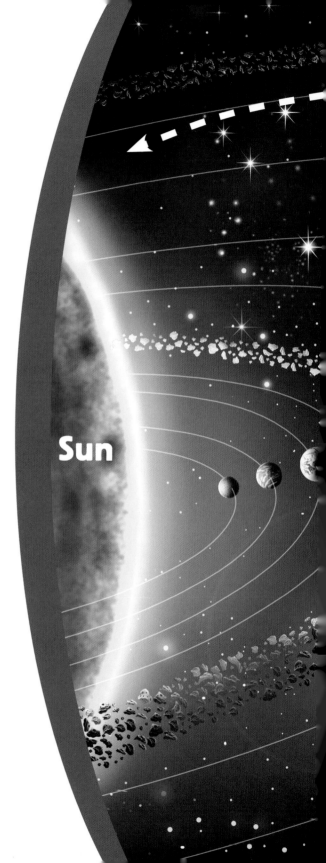

Sun

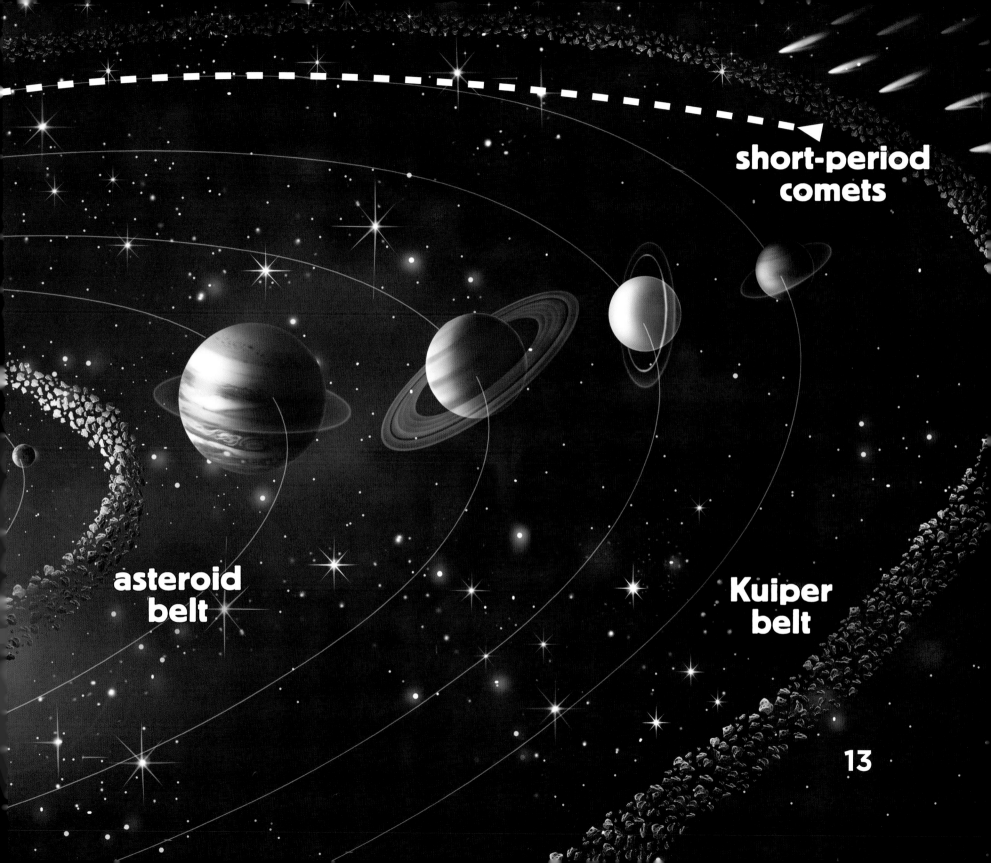

short-period
comets

asteroid
belt

Kuiper
belt

13

Long-period comets have **orbits** that take more than 200 years to complete. They come from the **Oort cloud**. Both kinds of comets travel near the sun at some point in their orbits.

14

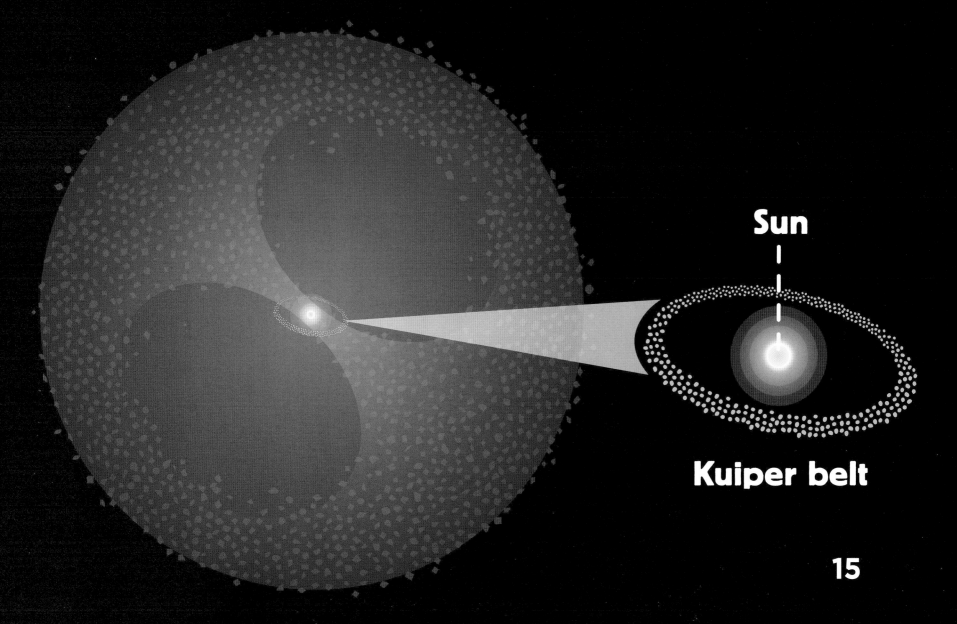

Oort cloud

Sun

Kuiper belt

Comas

When a comet nears the sun, it heats up. The heat makes the ice turn to gas. A cloud of dust and gas surrounds the nucleus. This is called a coma.

17

The coma keeps growing.
Solar winds push the coma
away from the sun. This creates
two tails. The dust and gas
make different tails. Tails can
spread for millions of miles!

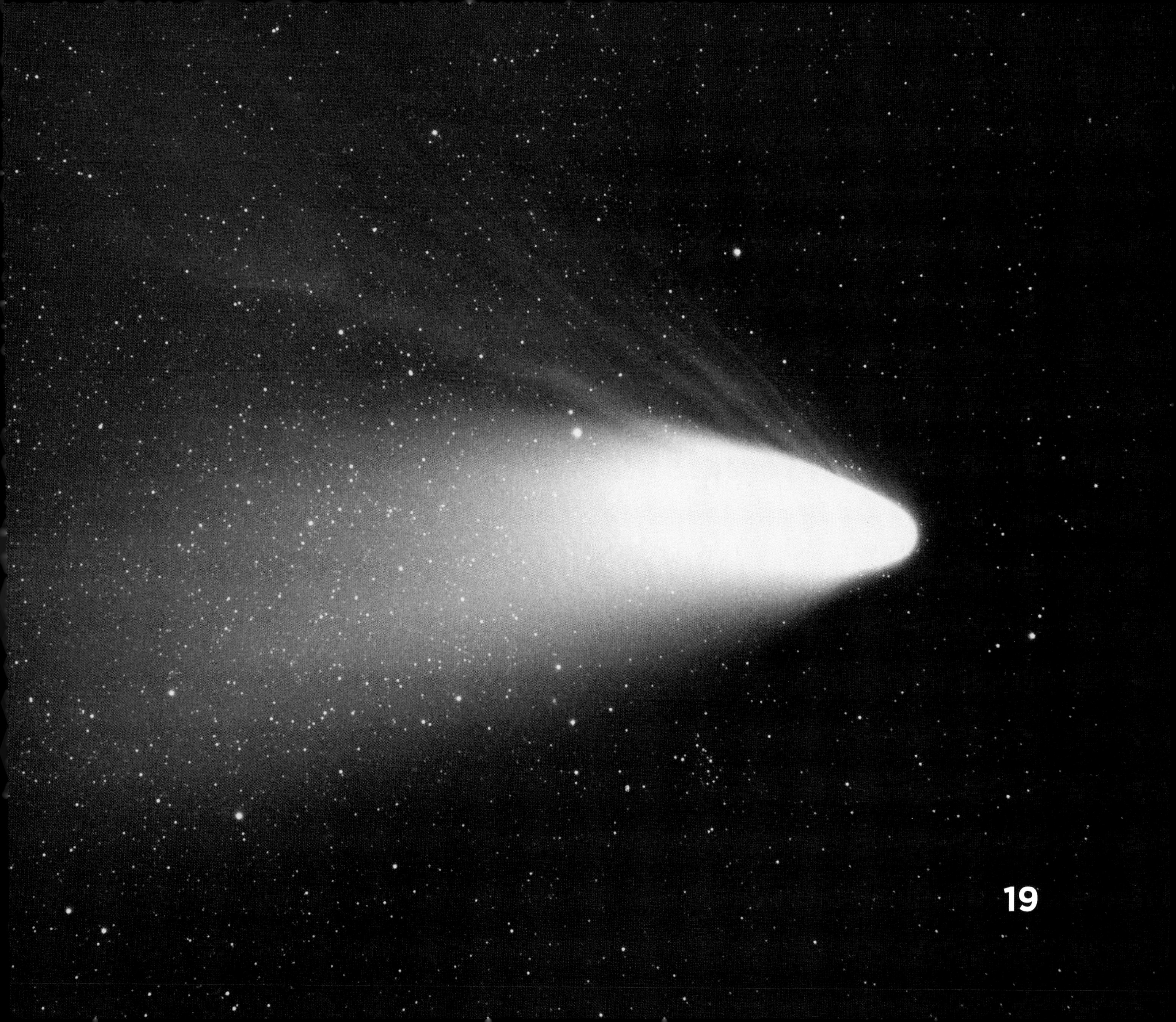

Sun Grazers

Most comets **orbit** far enough from the sun to pass safely. They move on to form icy rocks again. But some comets get too close. They completely **evaporate** or crash into the sun!

21

More Facts

- There are billions of comets in the Oort cloud and Kuiper belt.

- One of the most famous comets is Halley's Comet. It is a short-period comet that is visible from Earth every 75-76 years. The next time it will appear will be in the year 2061.

- Scientists sometimes refer to comets as dirty snowballs.

Glossary

evaporate – to change from a liquid or solid state into vapor.

nucleus – the solid, central part of a comet.

Oort cloud – a region of the solar system far beyond the planets in which billions of comets move in nearly circular orbits.

orbit – the curved path of a planet, moon, or other object around a larger celestial body.

scattered disc – an area filled with comets that is between the Kuiper belt and the Oort cloud.

solar system – a group of planets and other celestial bodies that are held by the sun's gravity and revolve around it.

solar wind – the constant stream of charged particles given off by the sun at high speeds.

23

Index

abdokids.com

Use this code to log on to abdokids.com and access crafts, games, videos and more!

Abdo Kids Code:
OCK0505

3 1333 04776 3899